A Concise
Introduction
to OS/2

GW00976239

ALSO AVAILABLE

A Concise
Introduction
to OS/2

by
Noel Kantaris

BERNARD BABANI (publishing) LTD.
THE GRAMPIANS
SHEPHERDS BUSH ROAD
LONDON W6 7NF
ENGLAND

PLEASE NOTE

© 1989 BERNARD BABANI (publishing) LTD

First Published – March 1989

British Library Cataloguing in Publication Data:
Kantaris, Noel
  A concise introduction to OS/2.
  1. Computer systems. Operating systems:
  I. Title
  005.4'3

  ISBN 0 85934 205 0

Typeset direct from disc by Commercial Colour Press, London E7.
Printed and Bound in Great Britain by Cox & Wyman Ltd, Reading

ABOUT THE BOOK

To help the beginner, this concise guide to OS/2, has been written without any assumptions regarding the user's present expertise in other operating systems; it has an underlying structure based on "what you need to know first, appears first". Users of PC/MS-DOS will immediately detect a certain familiarity with OS/2 as a great deal of this new operating system is based on it. This is particularly true, if OS/2 is run in command line mode, that is, typing the various operating system commands at the prompt rather than using the Presentation Manager — the user friendly graphical interface common to the OS/2 operating system and the various program applications running under it.

This book does not seek to replace the documentation you receive with the OS/2 operating system, but only to supplement and explain it. The book covers both command line processing and OS/2's Presentation Manager which should be somewhat familiar to users of DOS version 4.0 as the menus employed in the DOS shell of that version of the operating system are consistent with those used in Microsoft Windows and, hence, similar but not identical to those in OS/2's Presentation Manger.

This concise guide was written with the busy person in mind, by keeping its length to a minimum. It is hoped that with the help of this concise book you will be able to get the most out of your computer in terms of efficiency and productivity, and that you will be able to do it in the shortest, most effective and informative way.

ACKNOWLEDGEMENTS

I would like to thank colleagues at the Camborne School of Mines for the helpful tips and suggestions which assisted me in the writing of this book.

TRADEMARKS

ABOUT THE AUTHOR

Graduated in Electrical Engineering at Bristol University and after spending three years in the Electronics Industry in London, took up a Tutorship in Physics at the University of Queensland. Research interests in Ionospheric Physics, lead to the degrees of M.E. in Electronics and Ph.D. in Physics. On return to the UK, he took up a Post-Doctoral Research Fellowship in Radio Physics at the University of Leicester, and in 1973 a Senior Lectureship in Engineering at The Camborne School of Mines, Cornwall, where since 1978 he has also assumed the responsibility of Head of Computing.

CONTENTS

INTRODUCTION

Most 16-bit microcomputers use Microsoft's Disc Operating System (MS-DOS) as the prime means of interaction between user and computer. Owners of IBM personal computers (PCs), know this operating system as PC-DOS or DOS, which is IBM's implementation of MS-DOS. OS/2 is the natural successor to PC/MS-DOS and as such it should be seen within the context of the PC/MS-DOS cycle of development.

Since its inception in 1981, PC/MS-DOS has been the standard operating system for personal computers and by now is being used by more than 10 million people. As the number of users increased over the years, so too has the complexity of applications run on their PCs. To meet these ever increasing demands, PC/MS-DOS has also increased its functionality several times in the form of *new* versions, as shown in the table below.

Version	Date	Main changes in functionality
1.0	1981	Original Disc Operating System
1.25	1982	Support for double-sided discs
2.0	1983	Support for sub-directories
2.25	1983	Support for extended character set
3.0	1984	Support for 1.2MB floppy disc and larger capacity hard disc
3.1	1984	Support for PC networks
3.2	1986	Support for 3" floppy disc
3.3	1987	Support for PS/2 range of computers
4.0	1988	Support for extended memory (EMS), hard disc partitions beyond 32MB and a graphical interface DOS shell

One aspect of version 4.0 of the PC/MS-DOS operating system makes it different from earlier versions. This is the result of the addition of a DOS shell — a menu-driven graphical interface — which makes this version easier to use for the newcomer to the DOS environment. The menus employed in the DOS shell are consistent with those used in Microsoft Windows which makes it easier for those who become familiar with it to use the OS/2's Presentation Manager. As OS/2 will only run on PCs based around the 80286 and 80386 processors, the millions of users with machines based on the 8086 and 8088 processors will be confined to DOS, with version 4.0 providing the closest link to OS/2.

In April 1987, IBM introduced a new line of microcomputers, based mainly around the 80286 and 80386 processors (models 50 and above), under the name of *Personal System 2* (PS/2). Even though model 30 of the series was introduced at the time as a PS/2 model, the standard version of this model has an 8088 processor and, therefore, can't run the new OS/2 operating system which was also announced at the same time, but did not become available until a year later. In October 1988, IBM introduced a new version of model 30, the 30/286, with an 80286 processor, which is capable of running OS/2.

OS/2 provides a true multitasking environment. Multiple processes can run at the same time, protected from mutual interference, but able to communicate between them. DOS, on the other hand, is a single process (task) operating system and will remain as such. Users who move from DOS to OS/2 can use their DOS applications under the new operating system, provided they are happy to run them in the so-called 'compatibility box'. Such applications cannot multitask in the box, and if they are switched to background processing, they stop. Other software that cannot be run in the box are copy-protected applications and certain communications packages.

The advantage of multitasking can only be appreciated by anyone who has been in the middle of one computer program, say writing a report by using a word processor, and needing to include comparative figures from another program, such as a spreadsheet. Without multitasking the user has to exit the word processor, run the spreadsheet program, do the required 'what-if' calculations, make notes of the result, and return to the word processor in order to continue with the report writing. Under OS/2, multiple processes can run concurrently and can be grouped under 'sessions', thus allowing the user to switch easily from one session to another. Additionally, communication between processes, for data interchange, is made easy via a common memory area, called the 'clipboard'.

OS/2 v1.0 allows the control of multiple tasks through the Program Selector which offers the user two menus, a 'start list' showing programs which are available to be run, and a 'switch list' showing currently running programs, referred to as applications. Programs can be added to, or deleted from, the start list via a pull-down menu. Switching between application programs can be achieved with the use of the **Alt-Esc** key combination, which jumps to a different virtual screen, corresponding to a different running application. The **Ctrl-Esc** key combination returns the user back to the Program Selector, so that a new application can be chosen.

The current version of OS/2 comes in two options; the Standard Edition 1.1 and the Extended Edition 1.1, the difference being that the latter includes a database and communications software. Both options come with the new graphical user interface, called Presentation Manager, which is based on Microsoft Windows and is similar to the DOS v4.0 shell. Presentation Manager will run as an additional process, overseeing the applications running in the various windows, thus replacing the Program Selector. However, it is possible to use OS/2 without the Presentation Manager which will most likely be welcomed by current users of DOS who are familiar with command line processing, because using the Presentation Manager requires vast amounts of both computer memory and hard disc storage space. For this very reason, OS/2's commands are presented here first, while discussion on the use of Presentation Manager is deferred until later.

It is assumed here that the reader is familiar with handling floppy discs, floppy and hard disc drives and that the installation manual which comes with every microcomputer has been read and complied with. What this book tries to do is supplement the OS/2 operating manual by explaining the various commands with ample working examples which is something that such manuals seldom seem to do. They are excellent for reference purposes for those who already know, but learning from them is almost impossible.

The OS/2 operating system consists of a collection of small, specialised programs that make up the working environment which allows you to create and save programs, copy or delete data files from disc or perform other input and output (I/O) operations, such as finding a program or a file on a given disc or printing the contents of that file on the printer. In general, OS/2 is the microcomputer's administrator and understanding the way it works is very important.

At first, the various commands within OS/2 might appear difficult to understand and remember. However, there is a certain simplicity in the OS/2 command structure and once this is understood, using it becomes natural. This book seeks to bring to the forefront this inherent simplicity in OS/2 by presenting the principles of what you need to know, when you need to know them. At the same time, the book has been written in such a way as to also act as a reference guide, long after you have mastered its commands. To this end, a summary of the commands supported by OS/2 is given in the last-but-one section of this book. The commands are explained with relevant examples and, as such, the section can serve as a quick reference guide.

The Structure of OS/2

To understand how to use most effectively the OS/2 operating system, you must understand its underlying structure. The various OS/2 administrative functions are contained in four separate main files. These are:

OS2DOS.COM
OS2BIO.COM
CMD.EXE
COMMAND.COM

or IBMDOS.COM, IBMBIO.COM, CMD.EXE and COMMAND.COM in the case of the IBM product.

The first two files are hidden, so they do not appear on directory lists and cannot be deleted. The first file is the core of the OS/2 Disc Operating System, while the second one, also known as the Basic Input Output System (BIOS), allows the core to communicate with the hardware. It is the BIOS that can normally be adapted by various manufacturers of non-IBM hardware, so that the operating system can appear to function in the same way, even though there might be differences in hardware design. The third file, CMD.EXE, is the OS/2 Command Processor which analyzes what is typed at the keyboard, and if correct, finds and starts execution of the appropriate command. The last file, COMMAND.COM, allows the user to run DOS programs under real mode in the compatibility box.

OS/2 has over twenty built-in commands, normally referred to as 'internal commands', instantly available to the user as they reside in memory. In addition to these internal commands, there are over fifty 'external' commands which are to be found on the System and Utility discs supplied by the manufacturer of the operating system. The machine program which makes up each of these external commands is saved in a *file* under an appropriate name with a .COM or .EXE extension to the filename (more about this later). Collectively, these internal and external commands make up the microcomputer's Operating System. These commands will be examined in detail in the following sections of this book.

Booting up the System

To start up the computer, usually referred to as booting up the system, the OS/2 disc which contains the System files

4

(known as the System disc), must be in the A: drive, if the system is to be booted from the floppy disc, or the files must have been transferred on the C: drive, if the system is to be booted from the hard disc.

It is assumed here that you have followed the manufacturer's instructions (a) on how to format the hard disc and install OS/2, if you are a first-time user; or (b) if you are an existing DOS user and need to use DOS programs that may not run under OS/2 (such as communications and real-time programs or hardware dependent programs), you have a \DOS sub-directory with all your DOS files in it and have prepared a bootable floppy disc with your DOS System files on it (together with your **autoexec** and **config** files), before installing OS/2, so that in future you can boot up your system under DOS from the floppy drive. If either of these has not been done, then do so now, before going on any further.

In addition to the four special files in the System disc, there are a number of other files (over 50) supplied with the OS/2 system disc, which perform various important tasks. These files are collectively known as the OS/2 utilities and will be examined in detail later. To be able to distinguish between disc drives, OS/2 refers to them by a letter followed by a colon, e.g. A: or C: for the floppy and hard disc drive, respectively. An additional, internal or external floppy disc drive is refered to as the B: drive, while users on networked systems can access a network hard disc by assigning it as another drive on their microcomputer, namely as E: or Z:

On booting up the microcomputer from an OS/2 system disc, the following tasks are performed:

(a) A self test on its Random Access Memory (RAM) is performed

(b) A check is made to see if a floppy disc is in drive A:, and if there is, it checks to see if it is a system disc. If it is, it boots the system from the A: drive

(c) If no floppy exists in the A: drive, an attempt is made to boot the system from the C: drive, if there is one.

(d) Configures the system by executing the CONFIG.SYS file, if one exists, otherwise invokes the Program Selector

5

(e) Reads the BIOS and the OS/2 disc operating system files

(f) Loads into RAM the CMD.EXE file to make available the protected-mode command-line processor

(g) Executes the commands within the STARTUP.CMD file, if one exists, otherwise it asks for the Date and Time which can be reset at this point. Pressing the Return key, confirms what is displayed.

Should you receive any error message while these tasks are being performed, you could restart the process, after rectifying the error, by pressing simultaneously the three keys marked **Ctrl**, **Alt** and **Del**. This will re-boot the system.

The Program Selector is a front-end shell accessed with the PROTSHELL command from within the CONFIG file of OS/2 v1.0 by loading the SHELL.EXE file. With OS/2 v1.1, the PROTSHELL command has been changed to direct the system to load the Presentation Manager front-end shell PMSHELL.EXE instead. Thus, Presentation Manager replaces the Program Selector. Both these shells will be discussed in some detail within separate sections of this book.

OS/2 has over twenty internal commands built into it. which are instantly available as they reside in memory. These are:

Command	Meaning	Command	Meaning
BREAK	Set Ctrl Break on/off	CD	Change directory
CLS	Clear Screen	COPY	Copy file(s)
DATE	Display/set date	DEL	Delete file(s)
DETACH	Set background mode	DIR	Display directory
DPATH	Set data-file path	ECHO	Set Echo on/off
EXIT	Exit Command level	MD	Make directory
PATH	Search set directories	PROMPT	Change promp
RD	Remove directory	REN	Rename file(s)
SET	Change parameters	TIME	Display/set time
TYPE	Display a file	VER	Display OS/2 version
VERIFY	Check disc writing	VOL	Display disc volume

These commands (to be explained later), together with the rest of the operating system, occupy several kbytes of RAM, as they are loaded into memory on booting up the system. The additional (over fifty) OS/2 external commands, reside on the system disc. These can only be invoked if that disc is available, or can be accessed directly from the C: drive (had the system been booted from the hard disc drive).

THE OS/2 PROGRAM SELECTOR

The OS/2 Program Selector, otherwise known as the Session Manager, oversees each program (session) and allows the user to switch from one session to another and view the output of each on the screen. When the system is installed and ready for use, it displays the following:

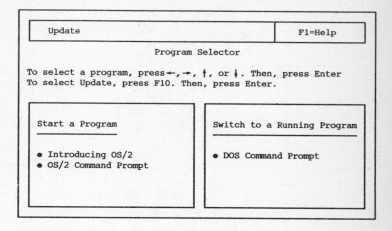

Choosing the first option from the menu under 'Start a Program', entitled 'Introducing OS/2' allows you to run a special demonstration program which goes through and explains many of the OS/2 functions.

Installing OS/2 Programs

Choosing the second option under the same menu, entitled 'OS/2 Command Prompt', allows you to start an OS/2 protected mode application. Choosing this option, the system displays the OS/2 command prompt [C:\] if the current drive is drive C. At this point, you can install your program by following its installation instructions, after which you should type

```
[C:\] EXIT followed by 'Enter'
```

to return to the Program Selector.

After installing OS/2 programs, you can include them within the menu under 'Start a Program' by pressing F10 followed by 'Enter' (or click mouse button 1) which selects 'Update' from the Program Selector. The screen will now look as follows:

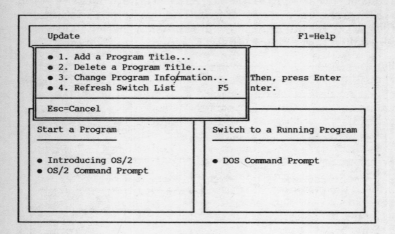

And selecting option 1, produces the 'Add a Program Title' screen on the display, as follows:

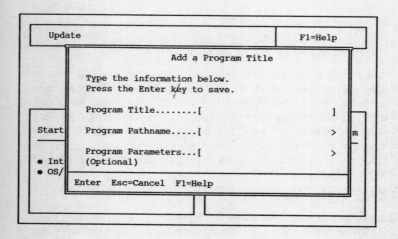

Program Title is the name you want listed under the 'Start a Program' menu option and must not exceed 30 characters,

Program Pathname is the drive, directory and filename of the program under consideration, and

Program Parameters are optional information which might be required with some programs in order to function under given hardware configurations.

Finally, pressing **Enter** adds the title to the Start a Program list and returns to the Program Selector menu.

Programs can be deleted from the Start a Program list by choosing option 2 from the Update menu. Option 3, allows us to change program information, while option 4, allows us to refresh the list of currently running OS/2 programs by deleting its name from the Switch to a Running Program list. This last option can also be selected by pressing F5 from the Program Selector.

OS/2 programs can be started in two ways: (a) by first adding the program title to the Start a Program list and then selecting it, in which case, and while the program is running, its name is automatically added to the Switch to a Running Program list, and (b) by selecting the OS/2 Command Prompt option and starting the program at the OS/2 command line, in which case, and while the program is running, the statement 'OS/2 Command Prompt #' is added to the Switch to a Running Program list. OS/2 programs run under a protected mode, thus allowing more than one program to run at the same time.

When a program ends, the system returns you to either the Program Selector or the OS/2 command prompt, depending upon where the program was started by method (a) or method (b), respectively. If the system returns you to the Program Selector, then its name is automatically removed from the Switch to a Running Program list. If the system returns you to the OS/2 command prompt, then type EXIT and press 'Enter' which causes the system to return you to the Program Selector and at the same time removes the 'OS/2 Command Prompt #' statement from the Switch to a Running Program list.

Installing DOS Programs

To install a DOS program, use the right arrow key to move the cursor to the 'Switch to a Running Program' and select the 'DOS Command Prompt' option. The system now displays the DOS prompt, namely

```
C:\>
```

if the current drive is the C: drive.

At this stage you must follow the installation instructions that come with your DOS program. After installation is completed, press the Ctrl-Esc key sequence in order to return to the Program Selector.

To start a DOS program which has already been installed, press the right arrow key to move the cursor to the Switch to a Running Program list and select 'DOS Command Prompt' and type the name that starts execution of the program. The program will be run in what is known as the compatability box in real mode. Only one DOS program can be run at a time.

OS/2 has kept complete DOS compatibility in its file system, so that DOS and OS/2 programs can both use the same files. Thus, files created by your DOS word processor (provided they are ASCII files) or from your DOS editor (such as **edlin**) can be read by OS/2 and acted upon. This will be of particular interest to current DOS users who can continue to use **edlin** or their favourite line editor to write the necessary files for configuring the system - more about this, later.

Files & the Disc Directory

To see what files are held on the System disc, select 'OS/2 Commmand Prompt' from the Program Selector, which will cause the OS/2 prompt to be displayed. At this point access the disc directory of the A: drive by typing

```
[C:\] DIR A: (and press the Enter key).
```

Amongst the many files to be listed, if the system disc was inserted in the A: drive before issuing the DIR command, will be the following:

Filename	Extension	Size	Date	Time
OS2BIO	COM	5120	27-05-87	12:00a
OS2DOS	COM	233016	27-05-87	12:00a
ANSI	SYS	1651	27-05-87	12:00a
CMD	EXE	56144	27-05-87	12:00a
COMMAND	COM	25839	27-05-87	12:00a
COUNTRY	SYS	14632	27-05-87	12:00a
FORMAT	COM			
INSTBOOT	CMD			
KEYBOARD	DCP			

Note that a filename consists of up to 8 alphanumeric characters (letters and numbers only) and has a three letter extension, separated from the filename by a period, i.e. COMMAND.COM or COUNTRY.SYS, without any spaces in between, unlike the listing appearing on your screen, where the periods have been omitted and the extensions have been tabulated. The size of each file (in bytes) is also given on the listing together with the date and time it was created.

The extensions .COM, .EXE and .SYS are the most common extensions of the files which make up the OS/2 operating system. They contain instructions which are executed directly by the computer. Other extensions commonly used by programs or users are:

.BAK   .BAS   .BAT   .CMD   .DAT   .DOC   .TXT   .TMP

which indicate "backup" files, "Basic" programs, "DOS batch" files, "OS/2 batch" files, "data" files, "document" files, "text" files and "temporary" files, respectively.

Returning to the result of issuing the DIR command; what is more likely to have happened in your case is that the listing of the first half of the files on your disc have scrolled out of view. In all, there are approximately fifty utility files on the System disc and you can only see the last twenty or so. To stop the scrolling of such a long directory, use the /P option after the DIR command, as follows:

```
[C:\] DIR A:/P
```

which will page the directory, displaying twenty files at a time. Alternatively, you could see all these files on your screen by using the /W option, as follows:

```
[C:\] DIR A:/W
```

which lists the files sideways, as shown below:

```
OS2BIO    COM   OS2DOS    COM   ANSI     SYS   CMD               EXE
COMMAND   COM   COUNTRY   SYS   FORMAT   COM   INSTBOOT   CMD
KEYBOARD  DCP
```

Note that in this case the information relating to the size of each file and the date and time of its creation has been omitted from the listing.

The slash (/) options in OS/2 commands, like the /P and /W in the DIR command above, are also referred to as switches. However, as this name could be confused with physical switches, the name options will be used throughout.

You can limit the information which appears on your screen by being more selective with the use of wildcards. For example, to list all the .EXE files on your disc, type

```
[C\] DIR A:*.EXE
```

where the wildcard character "*" stands for "all" files. Note that spaces are very important to OS/2. Had you not included a space after DIR in the above command, OS/2 would have responded with an error message.

The wildcard character "*" can also be used as part of the filename. For example,

```
[C:\] DIR A:CO*.*
```

will list all the files with all extensions on the A: drive, starting with the two characters CO, irrespective of the ending of the filenames.

The full OS/2 command should normally specify which drive you want to access, as shown above, but can be omitted if the command refers to the currently logged drive. Thus,

```
[C:\] DIR CO*.*         or
[C:\] DIR C:CO*.*       will access the specified files on the C: drive, while
[C:\] DIR A:CO*.*       will access the specified files on the A: drive.
```

Alternatively, you can change the logged drive by simply typing its identification letter at the prompt. For example,

```
[C:\] A:                will change the logged drive, indicated by changing
                        the prompt, to
[A:\] _
```

which indicates that the currently logged drive is now the A: drive. All further commands which do not specify a different drive, will access the A: drive. To revert back to the previously logged drive, type C: at the [A:\] prompt.

A more precise wildcard is the query character "?" which can be substituted for a single character in a filename. For example, assuming that there are several consecutively numbered files on your disc with filenames TEXT1.DOC to TEXT999.DOC, typing

```
[C:\] DIR TEXT?.DOC
```

will list all files with the extension .DOC, from TEXT1 to TEXT9, but not those within the range TEXT10 to TEXT999. On the other hand, using two consecutive query characters in the filename, such as

```
[C:\] DIR TEXT??.DOC
```

will list all files with the extension .DOC, from TEXT1 to TEXT99, but exclude those within the range TEXT100 to TEXT999.

To list all the files from TEXT1 to TEXT999 use the wildcard character "*" in place of the single query, as follows:

```
[C:\] DIR TEXT*.DOC
```

Finally, typing

```
[C:\] DIR *.*
```

will display all files with all extensions which, of course, has the same effect as typing

```
[C:\] DIR
```

Nevertheless, the *.* is worth noting as it is the most useful three-character combination in OS/2 and will be mainly used in housekeeping commands to be explained later.

Should you ever want to find out whether a particular file exists on a disc, just type its name after the DIR command. If the file exists, OS/2 will display it, otherwise the message

```
The system cannot find the file specified
```

will appear on your screen.

An enhancement to DIR under OS/2 protected mode, allows the placement of multiple file specifications on the command line. For example, the following command

```
[C:\] DIR *.DOC *.TXT
```

will cause OS/2 to use each file specification, one after the other, to perform multiple directory listings. First, all the files with the .DOC extension will be listed, followed by all the files with .TXT extension.

The command can also be extended to cover listings from different drives. For example,

```
[C:\] DIR *.DOC A:*.DOC
```

will first list all files with the .DOC extension from the C: drive, followed by all .DOC files from the A: drive.

MANAGING YOUR SYSTEM

OS/2 provides several commands which help you to manage your system and disc files efficiently. Some of these commands are internal and some are external. If the commands under discussion are external commands, it will be pointed out so you can insert the system disc in the logged drive which is the drive indicated by letter on the screen prompt.

The DATE Command:
Typing the command

```
[C\] DATE
```

at the prompt, evokes the response

```
Current date is dd/mm/yy
Enter new date:
```

at which point you can either type a new date or press Return to indicate that date is not to be changed. The above date format assumes that you have included the command COUNTRY=xxx, where xxx is a three digit code representing your country, in your CONFIG.SYS file (to be discussed later), otherwise the date will be shown in mm/dd/yy format.

The TIME Command:
Typing the command

```
[C:\] TIME
```

at the prompt, evokes the response

```
Current time is Hrs:Mins:Secs
Enter new time:
```

at which point you can either type a new time or press Return to indicate that time is not to be changed.

The FORMAT Command:
One of the first things you will need to do, as a new user, is to make a working copy of your System disc, or favoured software package, or just a backup copy of your programs or data. Such packages and/or data are far too valuable in terms of money or time invested in producing them to be used continually without the safeguard of backup copies. Again, it is assumed that in the case of a hard disc-based system, your hard disc has already been formatted according to your manufacturer's instructions when setting up the system.

A new floppy disc must be formatted before it can be used by your computer's operating system. A floppy disc that has been formatted in one computer, can only be used in another computer if they are compatible and use the same operating system.

To format a disc, in the case of a hard disc-based system, the logged drive will be C: and the new floppy disc is inserted in the A: drive. Now type the command

```
[C:\] FORMAT A:/S/V
```

Drive C: is accessed momentarily, the FORMAT utility file is loaded into RAM and executed. You are then given instructions to insert a floppy disc in drive A:, and press Enter to begin. Be very careful never to format an already formatted disc (particulary the C: drive), as *all* files that might be on it will be lost.

The /S option instructs OS/2 to copy all hidden system files, the OS2DOS.COM, OS2BIO.COM, CMD.EXE and COMMAND.COM files onto the newly formatted disc. This will be required if you intend to use the disc to boot up the system.

The /V option allows you to give a Volume label to your new disc, after formatting is completed.

There are some additional options that can be used with the FORMAT command which, however, are dependent on the type of disc drive being used and size of disc. These are as follows:

Disc type	Disc size	Parameters
360 kB	5.25"	/4
1.2 MB	5.25"	/4, /N, /T
720 kB/1.44 MB	3.5"	/N, /T

where

/4 formats 40 tracks with 9 sectors per track for 360 Kbytes using a 1.2 Mbyte high-capacity disc drive. This option must be used if you are using double-density and not high-capacity, double-density discs in a 1.2 Mbyte drive.

16

/N   specifies the number of sectors per track to format, written as /N:9 for nine sectors.
/T   specifies the number of tracks, written as /T:40 for forty tracks. To format a 720 Kbytes double-sided disc in a high-capacity 3.5" disc drive (1.44 Mbytes), use options /N:9/T:80.

If options /N or /T are specified, then both parameters must be entered. All other options can be used separately or omitted altogether from the command. Omitting the /S option from the FORMAT command saves disc space.

The SYS Command:
Should you change your mind after you have formatted a disc without the use of the /S option, you can use the external SYS command to transfer the System files from the logged disc drive onto a previously formatted disc, inserted in another drive. The command takes the form:

`[C:\] SYS A:`

To successfully transfer the operating system to a disc with this method, the disc must either be newly formatted or else have space on it for the transfer of the operating system by perhaps already having a different version of it on the target disc. Finally, note that the SYS command transfers only the two hidden files of the operating system which means that you must use the COPY command (see next section) to transfer the CMD.EXE, COMMAND.COM and CONFIG.SYS files.

Compatibility Between Double & High Density Discs:
Some compatibles have 360 Kbyte double-sided, double-density disc drives. Discs are formatted with 40 tracks per side, 9 sectors per track with 0.5 Kbyte of information per sector, resulting in 360 Kbyte capacity.

The AT, XT286 and some compatibles using the 80286 processor have 1.2 Mbytes double-sided, high-capacity disc drives. Discs are formatted with 80 tracks per side, 15 sectors per track with 0.5 Kbyte of information per sector resulting in 1.2 Mbytes capacity. However, each track takes the same physical space as that of the 360 Kbyte drive, the difference being that the 1.2 Mbyte drive writes tracks that are half the width of the 360 Kbyte drive.

Discs formatted on 1.2 Mbyte disc drives with the /4 option use only one half of the width of each of the 40 tracks. This information can easily be read by a 360 Kbyte drive (as a result of tolerance in signal level), provided the other

17

half of the track is completely clear. Should you now use the 360 Kbyte drive to write to the disc, information is written to the full width of the track which can still be read by the 1.2 Mbyte disc drive (again, as a result of tolerance in signal level).

However, any subsequent writing to such a disc using the 1.2 Mbyte drive, results in changes to only one half of the track width. The result is half a track containing the new information with the corresponding other half of the same track containing the old, half-overwritten information, which makes it impossible for the 360 Kbyte disc drive to make any sense of it.

There are no such compatibility problems arising from the use of 3.5" discs which have been formatted in 720 Kbytes capacity in a high-capacity (1.44 Mbytes) disc drive and subsequently used to read or write to them by either a 720 Kbyte or a 1.44 Mbyte disc drive.

The COPY Command:
To copy all files on the disc in the logged drive to the disc in the A: drive, type

```
[C:\] COPY *.* A:
```

Note the most useful three-character combination in OS/2, namely *.* which means "all filenames with all extensions".

However, if you wanted to copy a set of files from the A: drive to the C: drive, while being logged onto the C: drive, type

```
[C:\] COPY A:*.DOC C:
```

which means: COPY from the A: drive all files with extension .DOC to the C: drive.

The /V option can be used at the end of the COPY command to force OS/2 to verify that the file(s) it has copied can be read. For example,

```
[C:\] COPY FORMAT.COM A:/V
```

will copy the formatting utility file FORMAT.COM from the logged drive to the A: drive and force verification that the file can be read.

18

The DISKCOPY Command:
Both the formatting and copying can be done in one go by using the DISKCOPY command, as follows:

```
[A:\] DISKCOPY A:
```

which will copy all the files from from the source disc in the logged drive, in this case the A: drive, to the target disc in the A: drive and format the target disk at the same time. The operating system will inform you when to swap the target disc for the source disc in the A: drive.

The DISKCOMP and COMP Commands:
These two external utilities are mostly needed if you use the DISKCOPY command. The first one compares the contents of two discs, while the second one compares the contents of two files. The commands take the following form:

```
[C:\] DISKCOMP A: A:     compares the source and target discs in the A: drive
[C:\] COMP A:CMD.EXE      compares the CMD.EXE file to be found on the discs
                         in the C: and the A: drives
```

The DELETE Command:
Unwanted files on a disc can be deleted, as follows:

```
[C:\] DEL A:EXAMPLE.TMP    deletes EXAMPLE.TMP on the A: drive
[C:\] DEL EXAMPLE.TMP      deletes EXAMPLE.TMP on the C: drive
[C:\] DEL A:*.*            deletes all files on the A: drive!
```

Luckily, the use of the DEL *.* command evokes the response

```
Are you sure? (Y/N)
```

which acts as a safety net. It is a good idea to always check what you are about to DELete from your disc by first using the DIR command. For example, say you intend to DELete all the .TMP files from your disc. First use DIR *.TMP and if what is displayed on screen is what you want to DELete, then type DEL and press the F3 function key. This has the effect of displaying on the screen the last command you typed on the keyboard, minus the characters you typed prior to pressing the F3 key. Thus, DEL replaces DIR and the use of F3 displays the rest of the command. In this way you avoid making any mistakes by re-typing.

The RENAME Command:

The REN command is used to rename files. As an example, let us assume that we want to rename a file on the disc in the logged drive from its current filename OLDFILE.DOC to the new filename NEWFILE.DOC. This can be done as follows:

```
[C:\] REN OLDFILE.DOC NEWFILE.DOC
```

Note the importance of spaces after REN and in between the two file names. The command can be interpreted as:

Rename from filename1 to filename2

To rename a file on a disc in a disc drive other than the logged drive, the disc drive specification must also be included in the command, as follows:

```
[C:\] REN A:OLDFILE.DOC NEWFILE.DOC
```

Note that, if you intend to rename a file and give it a filename that already exists on disc, you must first delete the unwanted file before renaming, otherwise OS/2 will refuse to obey your command, informing you that the filename you have chosen already exists on disc.

The CHKDSK Command:

This command checks a disc, and reports on the original capacity of the disc, the number of bad sectors found on it, how much space they occupy and the remaining space available on it. The command also reports on the total number of files stored on the disc. The command takes the form:

```
[C:\] CHKDSK        which checks the disc in the logged drive, or
[C:\] CHKDSK A:     which checks the disc in the A: drive.
```

The additional /F option, allows CHKDSK to also do some routine maintenance, namely fixing lost clusters. A cluster is the minimum amount of space (one or more sectors) that can be allocated to a file on disc. Each disc has a File Allocation Table (FAT) where a note is kept of which clusters have been allocated to which file. However, with heavy disc use, the FAT can be corrupted and using CHKDSK will report "lost clusters found". The /F option, converts these into files and gives them the general name FILExxxx.CHK, where xxxx starts with 0000 and increments by 1. These files can then be checked for their content.

20

The TYPE Command:
This command allows you to see on screen the contents of text files. The command takes the form:

```
[C:\] TYPE filespec
```

This command is useful because it only lets you have a look at the contents of files without changing the environment in any way. For example, if you ever wanted to find out what is held in either the CONFIG.SYS or STARTUP.CMD files, then use this command rather than the editor.

If the text file you are looking at is longer than one screen full, then use **Ctrl-S** key sequence (while holding down the key marked **Ctrl**, press the **S** key once) to stop the scrolling of the display. Any key will start the display scrolling again.

Using TYPE on other than ASCII files (such as a .COM or .EXE file) could cause your system to "hang" as a result of attempting to display certain sequence of machine code that might be contained in the file. If that happens, use the **Ctrl-Alt-Del** key sequence to re-boot the system.

The TYPE command could be used to direct text files to the printer by typing

```
[C:\] TYPE EXAMPLE.TXT >PRN
```

where PRN stands for "printer" which is connected to the parallel printer port.

The VER Command:
To find out which version of OS/2 you are currently using, type

```
[C:\] VER
```

at the prompt.

The VOL Command:
To find out the volume label of the disc in the logged drive, type

```
[C:\] VOL
```

at the prompt. If the disc was not labelled during formatting, then the computer will respond with

21

```
Volume in drive C has no label
```

otherwise the appropriate label will be displayed.

The MORE filter Command:

This external filter command allows you to view text files a
page (23 lines) at a time — you are prompted to press a key to
display the next page. As such, it can be combined with
other commands to control scrolling of long ASCII files. For
example,

```
[C:\] TYPE EXAMPLE.TXT |MORE
```

or even used by itself (giving quicker response) as

```
[C:\] MORE<EXAMPLE.TXT
```

can help you with viewing long text files if you are not used
to or quick enough to use the **Ctrl-S** key sequence to halt
scrolling, after issuing the TYPE command.

The SORT filter Command:

One of the ways in which this external command can be
used is to sort and display alphabetically the contents of a
directory. For example,

```
[C:\] DIR |SORT
```

will sort the contents of the logged directory, including the
header and footer information, and display the result. For
long directories, use this command together with the MORE
filter, as follows:

```
[C:\] DIR |SORT |MORE
```

to display the sorted directory a page at a time.

A hard copy of the sorted directory of a disc could be
obtained by typing

```
[C:\] DIR |SORT >PRN
```

which re-directs output through the parallel printer port.

The PRINT Command:

The first time this command is used it has to be loaded into
memory as it is an external OS/2 command. However, from
then on it resides in memory and can be used without having
to re-load it.

The Print command provides background printing, that is, it can print long files while you are doing something else with your computer. In fact, using this command provides you with a print spooler which allows you to make and control a queue of several files for printing. The command takes the form:

```
[C:\] PRINT filespec        adds filespec to print queue
[C:\] PRINT filespec /C     cancels printing that file
[C:\] PRINT /T              terminates all printing
[C:\] PRINT                 displays files in queue
```

The PRINT command assumes that you have continuous paper in your printer. There is no facility to pause printing.

To print the two text files TEXT1.DOC and TEXT2.DOC, type

```
[C:\] PRINT TEXT1.DOC
[C:\] PRINT TEXT2.DOC
```

Wildcard characters can also be used in the command, as follows:

```
[C:\] PRINT TEXT*.DOC
```

which will spool all the files starting with the characters TEXT and having the extension .DOC to the printer.

The PRTSC Command:
Text which is displayed on the screen can be sent to the printer by pressing the Print Screen (**Shift PrtSc**) key.

On the other hand, pressing the **Ctrl** and **PrtSc** keys simultaneously causes re-direction of output to the printer. To cancel the effect, repeat the same key stroke.

The BACKUP and RESTORE Commands:
The external BUCKUP command allows you to archive files from the hard disc. Since your disc contains valuable work, you must make additional copies of all your important files. The BACKUP utility allows you to generate those backup copies on floppy discs. You should use this utility often; daily if necessary, depending on the amount of data you are generating. The command takes the form:

BACKUP *source destination options*

where   *source* is the drive/path/files to be backed up,
           destination is the drive to backup to, and
           options are:

23

/A to add the files to a disc in the destination drive
/D:date to backup only files from the specified date
onwards
/M to backup only files modified since they were last
backed up
/S to also backup sub-directories (see next section)
of the source path.

Thus, to backup, for the first time, all the word processor files whose path is \DATABASE\WPFILES, we type

```
[C:\] BACKUP C:\DATABASE\WPFILES\*.* A:
```

while to backup only files modified since they were last backed up, we type

```
[C:\] BACKUP C:\DATABASE\WPFILES\*.* A:/M
```

In both cases, the wildcard characters *.* ensures that all files with all their extensions in the WPFILES sub-directory are backed up.

The RESTORE external command allows you to de-archive files. It is the only utility which can restore to the hard disc files previously copied to floppy discs using the BACKUP utility. The command takes the form:

RESTORE *source destination options*

where   *source* is the drive to restore from,
          destination is the drive/path/files to restore, and
          options are:
          /P to prompt Y/N? before overwriting existing files
            by restoring, and
          /S to also restore files from sub-directories.

Thus, typing

```
[C:\] RESTORE A: C:\DATABASE\WPFILES\*.*/P
```

restores selected files from the floppy disc in the A: drive to the sub-directory WPFILES in the C: drive.

THE DIRECTORY TREE

If you are using a system with normal capacity disc drives, then organizing the files you keep on discs is relatively straightforward. The usual method would be to keep similar applications on the same disc, so that one disc might contain files on word processing, another on spread sheets, and another on databases. OS/2 keeps track of all such files by allocating space on each disc, called a directory, in which such information as the name of each file, its size, the date it was last amended, etc, is kept.

However, as you move up to systems with high capacity hard disc drives of 20 or more Mbytes, the amount of information you can store on them increases so much, that unless you organize the way you keep your files on such discs, you could easily spend all of your time trying to find one.

OS/2 can help you to organize your files on disc by providing a system of directories and sub-directories. The key to OS/2's system is the "root" directory, indicated by the back-slash sign (\), which is the main directory under which a number of sub-directories can be created. In turn, each sub-directory can have its own sub-directories, as shown below.

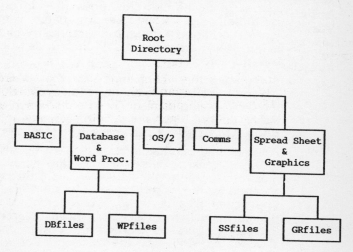

The root directory is shown here with five sub-directories under it, while two of these have their own sub-directories below them. For maximum efficiency, the root directory should contain only the System and start up files, together with information on its sub-directories, a kind of an index drawer to an office filing system.

Files in different sub-directories can have the same name because OS/2 can be told which is which via a system of PATH names. For example, a file in the SSFILES sub-directory could have the same name, say SALARY87.TMP, as one in the GRFILES sub-directory. Nevertheless, we can instruct MS-DOS to fetch the file in the SSFILES sub-directory by giving its path name which is:

`\SPREADSH\SSFILES\SALARY87.TMP`

whereas that of the file in the GRFILES sub-directory is:

`\SPREADSH\GRFILES\SALARY87.TMP`

In the example shown previously, the contents of the various sub-directories might be as follows:

`\` The root directory which contains the hidden System files OS2DOS.COM and OS2BIO.COM, the Command Processors CMD.EXE and COMMAND.COM, the CONFIG.SYS file, the STARTUP.CMD and AUTOEXEC.BAT files, the names of all its sub-directories (five in our example), and a number of batch files (corresponding to the sub-directories) which allow direct access to the sub-directories from the root directory.

BASIC A sub-directory containing all the BASIC programs which came on your system disc and the OS/2 examples disc. These are files which either contain the letters BAS, for example BASICA or GWBASIC, or have a .BAS extension.

DATABASE A sub-directory containing a database with built-in word processor. Below this, there are two sub-directories; one for the database files (DBfiles), and one for the word processor files (WPfiles). The actual files in these two different sub-directories will most certainly have different extensions; perhaps .DBS for the DBfiles and .DOC for the WPfiles, but the exact extension will be dictated by the actual software package.

OS/2	A sub-directory containing all the MS-DOS files comprising the external OS/2 commands.
COMMS	A sub-directory containing communications programs, propriety backup software, etc.
SPREADSH	A sub-directory containing an integrated spread sheet and graphics package. Below this, there are two sub-directories, one for the spread sheet files (SSfiles), and one for the graphics files (GRfiles). Again, the actual files in these two sub-directories will have different extensions which more than likely will be dictated by the software package.

OS/2 provides three special commands for the creation and management of sub-directories. these are:

Command	Meaning	Example
MD	Make sub-directory	[C:\] MD \BASIC
CD	Change directory	[C:\] CD \BASIC
RD	Remove directory	[C:\] RD \BASIC

These will be explained in detail shortly, but before we go any further, it will be extremely useful and prudent to have a prompt which indicates in which directory we are at any given time. We can do this by changing the prompt from always being [C:\], to indicate the PATH. To achieve this, type

```
[C:\] PROMPT $P$G
```

which after pressing Return, will change the prompt to

```
[C:\]\> _
```

indicating that the current directory is the root directory, shown by the back-slash (\).

This change of the prompt is imperative because without it you could be copying files to the wrong sub-directory without realising it. This command should be included in both your STARTUP.CMD and AUTOEXEC.BAT files (to be discussed later) so that it can be executed on booting up the system.

Managing directories

Before a directory can be used, it must exist. If it does not, you can make it with the MD command.

To make the sub-directory called BASIC, so that you could transfer to it all BASIC programs and files from your OS/2 system and utility discs, type the following line

```
[C:\]> MD \BASIC
[C:\]> _
```

which makes the BASIC sub-directory of the root directory and waits for further commands. Note that the full path was given after the MD command, by specifying first the root directory with the use of the back-slash (\) and then the sub-directory by its name.

To transfer files from a disc in the A: drive, first change directory using the CD command by typing

```
[C:\]> CD \BASIC
[C:\]BASIC> _
```

which causes the prompt to change, indicating that OS/2 has actually changed directory. Without the prompt change, you would have had the typical "where am I?" problem. Note that the moment we create a sub-directory we tend to refer to its parent as directory, even though itself might be a sub-directory to another parent directory.

To copy all BASIC programs and files to this directory, place in turn each OS/2 disc in the A: drive and type

```
[C:\]BASIC> COPY A:BAS*.*
[C:\]BASIC> COPY A:*BAS*.*
[C:\]BASIC> COPY A:*.BAS
[C:\]BASIC> _
```

Alternatively, we could have issued these commands from the root directory without first changing directories. As an example, the first line of the three copy commands given above, would have to be typed as

```
[C:\]> COPY A:BAS*.* C:\BASIC
```

which, however, involves more typing on your part.

Should you be dissatisfied with the name of a directory, you will have to make another directory giving it your preferred name, copy to it all files from the unwanted directory, delete all files from the unwanted directory, and then remove the unwanted directory from its parent directory. This procedure is essential because:

(a) you can not rename directories, and
(b) you can not remove directories unless they are empty.

As an example of the above procedure, let as assume that we have created, as discussed previously, a sub-directory to the root directory, called DATABASE. To have created such a sub-directory, we would have had to return to the root directory from whichever sub-directory we were at the time, by typing

```
CD \
```

at the prompt.

We now proceed to create a sub-directory to the DATABASE directory, called DOCBASE.

To create sub-directory DOCBASE, first change directory from the root directory to that of DATABASE, as follows:

```
[C:\]\> CD \DATABASE
[C:\]\DATABASE> _
```

then make a sub-directory called DOCBASE by typing

```
[C:\]\DATABASE> MD DOCBASE
```

at the prompt. Note that we have omitted the back-slash from in front of the sub-directory name which causes it to be made in the currently logged directory. Had we included the back-slash, the sub-directory DOCBASE would have been created as a sub-directory of the root directory.

Alternatively, we could make DOCBASE without first changing directory by issuing the MD command from the root directory, but giving the full path specification, as follows:

```
[C:\]\> MD \DATABASE\DOCBASE
```

Having made sub-directory DOCBASE, copy into it your files from the A: drive, as discussed previously.

29

Let us now assume that for some reason the directory name DOCBASE offends you and you would like to change it to WPBASE instead. To do this you will have to type in the following commands, assuming you are at the root directory.

```
[C:\]\> CD \DATABASE
[C:\]\DATABASE> MD WPBASE
[C:\]\DATABASE> CD \DATABASE\WPBASE
[C:\]\DATABASE\WPBASE> COPY \DATABASE\DOCBASE\*.*
[C:\]\DATABASE\WPBASE> CD \DATABASE\DOCBASE
[C:\]\DATABASE\DOCBASE> DEL *.*
Are you sure? (Y/N)Y
[C:\]\DATABASE\DOCBASE> CD \DATABASE
[C:\]\DATABASE> RD DOCBASE
[C:\]\DATABASE> _
```

In order of appearance, these lines of commands do the following:

(a) change directory to DATABASE
(b) make a sub-directory called WPBASE
(c) change directory to WPBASE
(d) copy from sub-directory DOCBASE all files to the logged sub-directory
(e) change directory to DOCBASE
(f) delete all files from logged directory
(g) OS/2 asks for confirmation
(h) change directory to DATABASE
(i) remove sub-directory DOCBASE.

As you can see, the procedure is cumbersome, so think how you want to structure your hard disc before plunging into it blindly.

Re-structuring directories and sub-directories, moving files from one sub-directory to another, or making backups of groups of files, can be made easy if you use certain propriety software. Such utilities can save you hours of effort and frustration and are well worth the very small initial outlay.

THE LINE EDITOR

OS/2 provides you with its own simple line editor, called **edlin**, and you should become familiar with its use. In general, **edlin** allow the creation and editing of ASCII files. These are text files which when sent to the screen or printer are interpreted as text.

Edlin can also be used to create the source code of various programming languages, such as Fortran and C. In such cases, remember to give the file the appropriate extension. For the two languages mentioned above, these will be **.for** and **.c**, respectively.

To invoke editor, the OS/2 system disc or a disc that contains it must be in one drive, and the file you want to create or edit must be specified. Thus, typing the command:

```
[C:\] edlin test.txt
```

expects to find both **edlin** and the fictitious file **test.txt** on the disc in the logged drive (in this case C:), while typing

```
[C:\] edlin A:test.txt
```

expects to find **edlin** on the disc in the logged drive and the file **test.txt** on the disc in the A: drive.

If the file does not exist on the specified disc, then **edlin** responds with

```
New File
*_
```

and waits for further commands, while if the file already exists, then **edlin** loads the file into RAM and responds with

```
End of input file
*_
```

Note the "*" prompt which is characteristic of **edlin**. Let us now create a text file, called **test.txt**, which we will use to demonstrate the power of **edlin**. To start, type at the OS/2 prompt

```
[C:\] edlin test.txt
```

which should cause **edlin** to respond with

```
New File
*_
```

if that file does not exist on your disc. If it does exist and you do not want to spoil its contents, then type **q** (for quit) and press the Return key.

The Insert Command on a New File
To insert lines of text, use the command **i** (for insert) at the prompt. In the case of a new file, as no lines of text exist in the file, type **1i** and then type in the short text given below.

```
*1i
        1:*first line of text
        2:*second line of text
        3:* ^C
*_
```

After typing **1i** at the prompt, **edlin** responds by giving a new line number (in this case 1:) with an asterisk after it to indicate that this is the current line. At this point we type 'first line of text'. On pressing the Return key, **edlin** gives us an additional line number, now 2:*, into which we type 'second line of text'. Again, on pressing Return, we are offered a further line number, and so on. To end the insertion mode, type **Ctrl-C**. The character ^C is the two-key depression **Ctrl-C** (hold the key marked **Ctrl** down and press the **C** key).

The List Command
To see what text is in the file, type **l** (for list) at the prompt, as follows:

```
*l
        1: first line of text
        2: second line of text
*_
```

The line numbers are inserted by **edlin** so that you can refer to the line you want to edit. Had you saved the file (see section on Exiting edlin), on listing, the first line would have been marked by an asterisk to indicate the current line. However, had you edited a line (see section on Edit), the last line edited would have become the current line and further attempts to list a very long file, would cause the current line to appear in the middle of the listing.

To list specific lines, use the **l** command with line numbers. For example,

```
*5,15l
```

will list lines from 5 to 15 inclusive. Note the syntax of the command which is: "From line number to line number Command". There must be no comma between the second line number and the command letter.

The Edit Mode

To edit a certain line in your file, type its line number and press Return. This puts you in edit mode and will cause the line whose number you typed to be displayed. Pressing Return again, confirms that you are happy with the contents of that line, otherwise you can either press the right cursor key to reveal each letter of that line, or re-type the entire line, making any necessary changes. In our case, we want to change line 2 to

```
second line of text, edited
```

so enter the edit mode and change the line appropriately. This is best done by using the right arrow cursor key to reveal the whole of the existing line and then typing the extra information at the end of it. The **Ins** and **Del** keys can also be used to edit the text.

The Insert Command on an Existing File

To insert lines of text, use the command **i** (for insert) at the prompt. However, be warned. Using i by its own will insert the new line before the current line (the one with the * after the line number). To insert lines at any other point, give the line number before the command.

In our case, we would like to insert two additional lines after the existing two. To do this, type

```
*3i
        3:*third line of text
        4:*fourth line of text
        5:* ^C
*_
```

Again, insertion mode is terminated in line 5: by pressing **Ctrl-C.** If we now list the contents of the file, we get:

```
*1
        1: first line of text
        2: second line of text, edited
        3: third line of text
        4: fourth line of text
*_
```

The Delete Command

To delete unwanted lines of text, use the **d** command (for delete) at the prompt. However, if you use the d command without any number associated with it, you will delete the current line (the one with the asterisk). Therefore, if you want to delete line 13, say, type

```
*13d
```

or if you want to delete a group of lines, type

```
*13,15d
```

which is translated as "lines 13 to 15 to be deleted".

The Move and Copy Commands

To move or copy text, use the **m** or **c** commands (for move or copy). These commands must be preceded by three numbers, as follows:

```
*13,15,8m
```

which is interpreted as "lines 13 to 15 to be moved to a position before line 8".

Similarly, the **c** command will copy a block and insert it before the given line. To move or copy a single line, the first two numbers in the command will have to be the same. After moving or copying lines, always use the list command to force renumbering of the file's contents.

The Search Command

To search for the occurrence of a word or a specified number of characters in a file you have created using **edlin**, use the search command. Just as in the list and delete commands, a line range is first specified, followed by the s (for search) command. Thus, typing

```
*1,4s edited
```

evokes the response

```
        2: second line of text, edited
*_
```

which displays the line containing the word 'edited'.

   Note that the space between the command s and the word 'edited' becomes part of the search string. Had we been searching for the characters 'con' within the word 'second', we would have had to omit the space between the command s and the string 'con'.

   The search command finds only the first occurrence of the specified string. To continue the search for further ocurrences of the same string, simply type **s** again. Thus, typing

```
*1,4sir
        1: first line of text
*s
        3: third line of text
*_
```

causes **edlin** to first find the string 'ir' in the word 'first' of line 1:, then by typing s again, it forces **edlin** to find the same string 'ir' in the word 'third' of line 3:.

The Search and Replace Command

This command is similar to the search command, except that it requires a replacement string. Thus, typing

```
*1,4r edited ^Z re-edited
```

will cause *all* occurrences of the word 'edited' to be replaced by the word 're-edited' in *all* the specified lines of text. Here, of course, it only occurs once in line 2: of the text. The character ^Z is the two-key depression **Ctrl-Z** (hold the key marked **Ctrl** down and press the **Z** key), which acts as a delimiter between the two strings. Again note that the space in front of both words becomes part of both the searching and the replacing strings.

The Transfer Command

This command transfers the contents of a file into the file currently being edited. The format of the command is:

[*n*] T *filespec*

where

n	specifies the line number where the new data is to be inserted. The data is inserted before the specified line. If the line number is omitted, then the current line is used.
filespec	specifies the file that you want to insert the contents of into the current file in memory.

Exiting edlin

To end the current session and exit **edlin** at any point, type

*e

which saves a new file under the chosen filename.

However, if the filename already existed on disc prior to using **edlin**, ending **edlin** has the following effect:

First the name of the old file on the disc is given the extension **.bak**, then the new file you have created by editing the old one is saved with the original extension. In this way you can make mistakes without disastrous effects since the system makes a backup file of the original. If need be, you could DELete the **.txt** file and then REName the backup file (**.bak**) to its original name and extension.

Note that **edlin** is disciplined not to allow editing of backup files so, should you want to start using **edlin** to edit the contents of a **.bak** file, you must first rename it, by giving it a different extension, before proceeding.

If, on the other hand, you realised that too many mistakes were made during editing, you could use the **q** command to quit, as follows:

*q

instead of using the **e** command as discussed above. Doing this causes **edlin** to ask you whether you want to abort. Typing **y** (for yes), leaves the name and contents of the original file on disc unaltered.

The **edlin** line editor supports some extra commands which were not discussed here. The commands presented are more than enough for writing and editing all but the most difficult programs. If you intend to write complicated programs which might require extensive editing, then it is best to use a full screen editor or your word processor, provided, of course, it can export files in ASCII format.

SYSTEM CONFIGURATION

The CONFIG file

This file allows you to configure your computer to your needs, as commands held in it are executed during system boot up. Each time the system is booted, the OS/2 start-up procedures search in the root directory on the logged drive for the CONFIG.SYS file if only OS/2 has been installed, or CONFIG.OS2 if DOS has also been installed in a dual-boot system. If the file is found, then the instructions within it are executed, thus configuring the system acordingly. If, however, OS/2 does not find this file, it uses its default values to configure the system.

As the CONFIG.SYS file is an ASCII file, the easiest way to create it or amend it is with the use of the editor, as discussed in the previous section. Do remember, however, that if your system has already been implemented by your computing staff, this file has already been written and you must not use the editor to look at its contents (use instead the **type** command), unless you have to and you know precisely what you are doing, as the file contains entries that OS/2 uses to define specific operating attributes.

OS/2 allocates memory space in RAM, called buffers, during installation (rather than from within the CONFIG.SYS file which has been the case with DOS) to store whole sectors of data being read from disc. If more data are required, OS/2 first searches the buffers before searching the disc, which speeds up operations. The installed number of buffers can be changed by filling in a configuration screen. However, as each buffer requires an additional 0.5 Kbyte of RAM, the number you should use is dependent on the amount of available memory. Best results are obtained by accepting the OS/2 default value.

Following is a list of the commands that you can include within the CONFIG.SYS file which OS/2 supports. However, do remember that any changes made to this file only take effect after re-booting which can be achieved by pressing the three keys marked **Ctrl**, **Alt** and **Del** simultaneously. A brief explanation of the commands is also given.

BREAK   By including the command BREAK=ON in the CONFIG.SYS file, you can use the key combination **Ctrl-C** or **Ctrl-Break**, to interrupt OS/2 I/O functions when operating in real mode. In protected mode the BREAK is always ON.

COUNTRY   OS/2 displays dates according to the US format which is month/day/year. To change this to day/month/year, use the command

```
COUNTRY=044
```

where 044 is for U.K. users. Non U.K. users can substitute their international telephone country code for the 044. The default value is 001, for the USA.

CODEPAGE   The table that OS/2 uses to define a character set is called a code page. Thus include the command

```
CODEPAGE=437
```

where 437 is the code page definition of pre-3.3 versions of DOS. In PC-DOS 3.3 the extended IBM character set was changed to accommodate different versions of it by offering several choices on the characters displayed or printed. If you are a newcomer to OS/2, then use the multilingual code page 850 in which many of the scientific symbols and box graphic characters have been replaced by international characters. This allows more Europian languages to be supported.

However, using any other than code page 437 might cause problems with some application programs running under DOS as not all would have adapted to the new codes. For more details regarding the new code page numbers and the requirment of using the DEVICE= statement in the CONFIG.SYS file when the new codes are being used, see your OS/2 reference guide. No additional DEVICE= statements are required with code page 437.

DEVICE   OS/2 includes its own standard device drivers which allow communication with your keyboard, screen and discs. However, these drivers can be extended to allow other devices to be connected by specifying them in the CONFIG.SYS file. Example of these are:

```
DEVICE=ANSI.SYS
```

which loads alternative screen and keyboard drivers for ANSI support for OS/2 real mode — features of which are required by some commercial software.

```
DEVICE=MOUSEAnn.SYS
```

allows the use of specific mouse devices.

If an IBM mouse is fitted, then the supplied MOUSE.COM file should be copied into the \OS2 sub-directory. The command MOUSE should then be inserted in the STARTUP.CMD and AUTOEXEC.BAT files, instead of the DEVICE= command in the CONFIG.SYS file.

```
DEVICE=DRIVER.SYS
```

allows you to connect an external disc drive.

```
DEVICE=EGA.SYS
```

provides mouse support for EGA modes.

```
DEVICE=COMn.SYS
```

specifies asynchronous drivers for the serial ports, where for n=01 specifies an IBM PC AT COM device, and n=02 specifies an IBM PS/2 COM device.

DEVINFO   Specifies the devices for which the code pages will be used.

LIBPATH   Specifies the path searched for the OS/2 dynamic-link libraries.

PROTSHELL Defines the protected-mode command-line interpreter.

RMSIZE   Specifies the number of kilobytes that OS/2 allocates for real-mode processing.

RUN   Allows you to execute a background task during system startup.

SWAPPATH   Defines the location that OS/2 uses for swapping files from memory to disc.

39

The STARTUP.CMD

This file is a special batch file that OS looks for during the last stages of a boot and if the file is not found, it displays the Session Manager. However, if the file exist in the root directory, the commands held in it are executed. One such command is the KEYBxx which configures keyboards for the appropriate national standard, with xx indicating the country. For the U.K., the command becomes KEYBUK, and you will need to execute it if your keyboard is marked with the double quotes sign on the 2 key and/or the @ sign over the single quotes key and/or the £ sign over the 3 key. To create the STARTUP.CMD file, use the editor as discusserd earlier, and include the command

```
KEYBUK
```

There are a lot of other commands that can be included in the STARTUP.CMD file, such as setting the PATH, changing directory or executing a program. Such commands will be discussed in detail in the next section. However, in the mean time remember to re-boot the system in order to activate the STARTUP.CMD file after you have created it.

The AUTOEXEC.BAT file

As we saw above, whenever OS/2 boots the system, it looks for the STARTUP.CMD batch file. Similarly, the first time you select the real mode session, OS/2 looks in the root directory for this other special batch file, called AUTOEXEC.BAT (users of DOS will be familiar with this filename). If the file exists, then the commands held within it are executed, otherwise OS/2 displays the real-mode prompt.

Again, as is the case with STARTUP.CMD batch file, there a lot of commands that can be included within AUTOEXEC.BAT and these will be discussed shortly when the concepts of batch files are introduced.

Simple batch files

Naturally, we would like to be able to use the OS/2 external commands from anywhere within the directory tree without having to specify where the commands are kept (in this instance, we have transferred them into the OS2 directory). The same could be said for the programs kept in the COMMS directory. This can be achieved by the use of the PATH command, as follows:

```
PATH C:\;C:\OS2;C:\COMMS
```

40

which should be included in the STARTUP.CMD file. Note the repeated reference to the C: drive which allows the path to be correctly set even if the user logs onto a drive other than C:.

By now you must have noticed that every time you boot up the system, the commands within your STARTUP.CMD file are echoed (displayed) onto the screen. To clean up the screen of such echoes, change your STARTUP.CMD file to include:

```
ECHO OFF
CLS
PATH C:\;C:\OS2;C:\COMMS
KEYBUK
PROMPT $P$G
ECHO HELLO ... This is your
VER
```

which has the following effect. First echoing is switched off, but only after executing the ECHO OFF command and thus, to clear the screen of the displayed command, we employ the CLS command. Then, the path, keyboard and prompt commands are executed unseen, until echo is re-activated by executing the ECHO command with a trailing message which is displayed on the screen, followed by the version (VER) of the OS/2 operating system.

To complete the implementation of the hard disc, we need to create a few batch files in the root directory which will help to run the system efficiently. For example, we might require to know the exact name of a OS2 or a COMMS command. This can be arranged by creating a batch file for each to display the corresponding directory, whenever the appropriate name is typed. As an example, we will use the editor to create the OS2.CMD file in the root directory, as follows:

```
ECHO OFF
CLS
CD \OS2
DIR/P
CD \
```

In line 3, the directory is changed to that of OS2 and line 4 causes the contents of the OS2 directory to be displayed using the paging (/P) option. Finally, line 6 returns the system back to the root directory.

Thus, typing OS2, displays the OS2 directory, while typing any external OS/2 command, invokes the appropriate command. A similar batch file can be built for displaying the COMMS directory, the only difference being in line 3, so that the correct directory is accessed and displayed.

Furthermore, it is most likely that the software packages you will be using in place of our imaginary DATABASE and SPREADSH packages (included as sub-directories to the root directory), require you to type their name in order to activate them. However, most packages also include a second file which is loaded from the first when its name is typed. In such cases you cannot use the PATH command within the STARTUP.CMD file to point to the particular package, as OS/2 will search for the second file in the root directory. To overcome this, you must use the APPEND command, as follows:

```
APPEND C:\;C:\DATABASE
```

and you must include it within the STARTUP.CMD file after the PATH command.

Finally, it would be ideal if the language BASIC could be accessed direct from the root directory. However, we can not include the BASIC directory in the PATH command of the STARTUP.CMD file, as we have done with the OS/2 and COMMS directories, because there might be three main versions of the BASIC language, say, BASIC, BASICA and GWBASIC. Instead, we have to create a rather special batch file in the root directory, again using the editor, as follows:

```
ECHO OFF
CLS
CD \BASIC
%1
CD \
```

Note the variable %1 in line 4 which can take the name of any of the three BASIC languages mentioned above, provided the appropriate variable name is typed after the batch file name. For example, typing

```
[C:\]> BAS GWBASIC
```

at the prompt, starts executing the commands within the batch file BAS.CMD, but substituting GWBASIC for the %1 variable. Thus, line 4 causes entry into GWBASIC, provided it exists in the BASIC directory. Similarly, typing

```
[C:\]\> BAS BASICA
```

causes entry into BASICA, again provided it exists in the BASIC directory.

Additional Batch-file Commands
Apart from the batch-file commands discussed already, there are a number of additional commands which can be useful when writing batch files. These are presented below.

Command   *Action*

FOR   Repeats the specified MS-DOS command for each 'variable' in the specified 'set of items'. The general form of the command is:

```
FOR %%variable IN (set of items) DO command
```

where 'command' can include any DOS command or a reference to the %%var. For example,

```
FOR %%X IN (F.OLD F.NEW) DO TYPE %%X
```

will display F.OLD followed by F.NEW

GOTO label   Transfers control to the line which contains the specified label. For example,

```
GOTO end
---
---
:end
```

sends program control to the :end label

IF   Allows conditional command execution. The generaal form of the command is:

```
IF [NOT] condition command
```

where 'condition' can be one of

```
EXIST filespec
string1==string2
ERRORLEVEL=n
```

Each of these can be made into a negative condition with the use of the NOT after the IF command.

43

REM	Displays comments which follow the REM
SHIFT	Allows batch files to use more than 10 replaceable parameters in batch file processing. An example of this is as follows:

```
:begin
TYPE %1 | MORE
SHIFT
IF EXIST %1 GOTO begin
REM No more files
```

If we call this batch file SHOW.BAT, then we could look at several different files in succession by simply typing

```
SHOW file1 file2 file2
```

as the SHIFT command causes each to be taken in turn.

PRESENTATION MANAGER

The OS/2 v1.1 comes with a PROTSHELL command that directs the system to load the PMSHELL.EXE (Presentation Manager) shell which replaces the Program Selector of version 1.0. Installing OS/2 v1.1 in place of the existing OS/2 v1.0 is quite straightforward. Unlike OS/2 v1.0, this version does not limit disc partitions to 32MB, so you might like to repartition your hard disc before installation. In this and some other respects, OS/2 v1.1 is similar to DOS v4.0. The user must, however, be warned that should the hard disc be repartitioned to greater than 32MB, then only DOS v4.0 would function correctly in a dual-boot system.

The installation process requires the user to respond to a few prompts and the process is completed by putting extra discs into the floppy disc drive. The whole system requires about 3MB of hard disc space. However, a more critical requirement is that the system needs at least 3MB of RAM to function fully, particularly if the DOS compatibility box is also installed. The system comes with an installed computer-based training program, so that users can teach themselves how to use it.

Presentation Manager has extended versions of the same functions as the Program Selector of v1.0; you can switch to a running program, get on-line help, start programs written for OS/2, or start a DOS application in real mode. Programs written for the Presentation Manager and most OS/2 v1.0 applications can be run within windows on the same screen (with movement between screens being achieved by typing the Alt-Esc key combination), while DOS and its applications always run in their own screen group, which means that the Presentation Manager graphics screen is replaced by a text-mode full screen and the familiar C:\> command prompt.

When the system is booted with OS/2 v1.1, the menu-driven graphics-based interface is activated showing the 'Start Programs' main window, as shown in Fig.1, which lists all the installed applications and allows access to either the OS/2 or the DOS command line. OS/2 programs can be activated from the 'Start Programs' window, while DOS programs can only be run from the command line. At the bottom of Fig. 1, there are three icons, two at the left corner representing the DOS compatibility box and print queue, and one on the right corner representing the 'Task Manager'. Any one of these can be activated by pointing to it with the mouse pointer and double clicking the mouse left button.

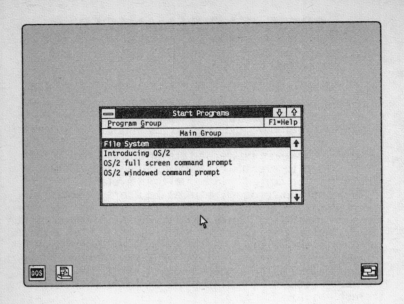

The Start Programs window has two options: 'Program' and 'Group'. The first allows a user to start, add, delete, etc., programs from the list, while the second option allows additional OS/2 programs to be installed in particular groups, so that different users can have their own menus. Installable programs are of three types; the first being one written specifically for Presentation Manager — employing its user interface functions and graphics capabilities, while the other two types are for OS/2 v1.0 applications.

The 'Task Manager' window lists active programs and lets the user switch between them: it provides three options: 'Control', 'Arrange' and 'Shutdown'. The first of these allows the user to switch between tasks and terminate programs, the second allows for the positioning of open windows on the screen, while the third option allows the user to log-off the system, but with the additional facility of permitting the current configuration of running programs to be saved so that on startup those applications can be loaded automatically.

The various options offered from the Start Programs and Task Manager windows are shown below in schematic form.

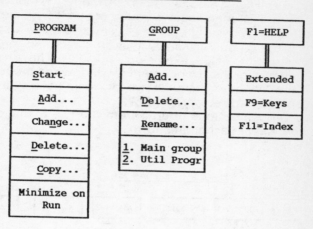

START PROGRAMS

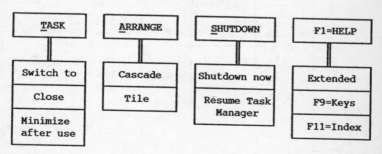

TASK MANAGER

To add a program to the current list, the full path to its executable file must be known. Should you be uncertain of this, the 'File System' can be used to locate the program file through its 'Tree' option.

Activating the 'Tree' option gives a representation of the hard disc's directory structure. A feature of this is that sub-directory structure can be contracted or expanded at will to help with searches.

The main window of the 'File System' displays six menus. These are: 'File', 'Options', 'Tree', 'Arrange', 'Window' and 'Exit'. The 'File' menu allows you to copy files, delete files, rename a file, move a file, print files, and so on. The 'Options' menu allows you to display files in directories ordered according to file name, extension, and so on. The 'Arrange' menu allows for the arrangement of windows on the screen, while the 'Window' menu allows for closing and switching between open directory windows.

The various options offered from the File Manager are shown below in schematic form.

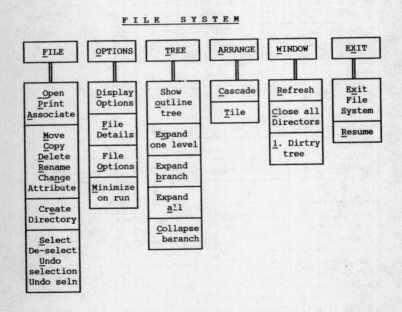

F I L E   S Y S T E M

Finally, the various global parameters to Presentation Manager can be set from a 'Control Panel' which is reached from 'Start Program' with the 'Group' option set to 'Utilities' and has three menus. The first, called 'Preferences', allows for control of screen colours, display border width, mouse control, etc., while the second, called 'Setup' allows the setting up of communication ports, printer defaults, spooler options, etc. The last menu, called 'Installation', allows the installation of fonts, printer drivers, and queue processor.

The various options offered from the Control Panel are shown below in schematic form.

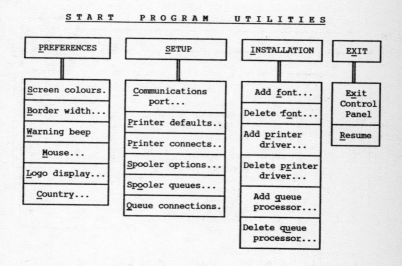

Presentation Manager also includes a 'clipboard' facility to which programs can write their output to, or from which programs can take their input as if it was supplied from the keyboard. This facilitates communication between different applications and together with the ability to run more than one program with a consistent user interface, makes it an invaluable operating system.

The System Editor

OS/2 v1.1 comes with its own screen editor, called the 'System Editor', which replaces the Edlin line editor of OS/2 v1.0. The System Editor provides you with text editing functions that let you create and edit files, get online help, copy blocks of information from one place to another, locate and change text automatically, and edit up to ten files simultaneously.

The System editor can be started from either the OS/2 command prompt by typing E, or from the Start Programs window using the mouse by clicking on 'Group', then 'Utility programs', and finally double clicking on 'OS/2 System Editor'. In either case, the 'Edit a File' window appears as shown below.

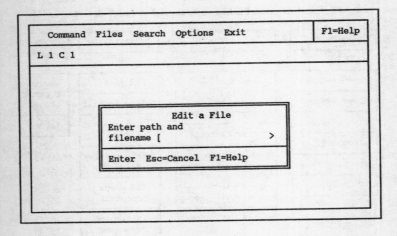

To create a file, type a filename in the 'Edit a File' window, and press the 'Enter' key. If the filename already exists, its contents will be displayed on the screen. The top line on the screen (reached by pressing F10) is the System Editor's action bar that contains keywords you can select. Selection of each keyword causes a list of options to be displayed on a pull-down menu. The area just under the action bar displays the line (L) and column (C) number where the text cursor is positioned, as well as the current filename. Online help makes this editor very easy to use.

COMMAND SUMMARY

The following is a summary of the commands supported by the OS/2 operating environment. For a fuller explanation of both commands and options, consult your system's OS/2 reference manual. The various commands are labeled internal or external, together with their mode, that is, protected or real, with external commands being accessible to the user only if the full filespec (drive and path) is given to were the appropriate command file resides.

Command	Explanation
ansi	Internal, protected — enables ANSI support for a protected-mode session, which can be turned ON or OFF. Omitting ON or OFF reports the current status.
	Example: ansi ON
	To provide ANSI support for real mode, the ANSI.SYS driver must be installed from within the CONFIG.SYS file with the DEVICE=ANSI.SYS command.
append	External, real — sets a path that OS/2 will search for files when they are not in the current directory. It can also be told not to search already defined paths.
	Example: append c:\wproc\docs
	searches the \wproc\docs directory on drive c: for files.
assign	External, real — assigns a drive letter to a different drive.
	Example: assign a=c
	allows all references to drive a: to go to the c: drive.

| attrib [options] | External, protected/real — sets or resets the 'read only' attribute and archive bit of a file, and displays the attributes of a file. |

Options:
+r sets read-only mode of a file
−r disables read-only mode
+a sets the archive bit of a file
−a clears the archive bit
/s processes all sub-directories

Example: attrib +R filespec /S

| backup [options] | External, protected/real — backs up one or more files from one disc to another. It can also automatically format the destination disc. |

Options:
/s backs up sub-directories also
/m backs up only those files that were changed since the last backup
/a adds files to be backed up to those already on the backup disc without erasing old files
/d backs up only those files which were modified after a given date
/l makes a backup log entry in a file called BACKUP.LOG
/t backs up only those files that were changed after a given time

Example: backup c:\ a:/s

backs up all files on the c: drive onto the a: drive.

| break | Internal, real — sets the Ctrl-C or Ctrl-Break option. |

Example: break ON

In OS/2 mode, the check for Ctrl-Break is always ON.

call

Internal, protected/real — allows a nested batch file to be invoked from within an OS/2 batch file.

cd (or chdir)

Internal, protected/real — changes the working directory to a different one.

Example: cd\wproc\docs

chcp [nnn]

Internal, protected/real — selects current code page for as many devices as possible. Omitting 'nnn' displays the current code page.

chkdsk [options]

External, protected/real — analyses the directories, files and File Allocation Table on the logged or designated drive and produces a disc and memory status report. It also reports the volume, serial number and disc allocation units.

Options:
/f fixes any problems found during the check
/v causes the display of filespecs as they are being processed

Example: chkdsk a:/f/v

cls

Internal, protected/real — clears the screen.

cmd [options]

External, protected — invokes a secondary command-line processor.

Options:
/c loads the secondary command processor only long enough to the command following it
/k loads the secondary command processor and after execution of the command following it leaves the secondary command processor in memory

Example: cmd /c chkdsk a:

This command, loads a secondary command processor, for long enough to executes the **chkdsk** command.

command [options]   External, real — starts the command processor. This is loaded into memory in two parts: the resident part and the transient part which can be overwritten by some programs in which case the transient part is reloaded.

Options:

/e:*n*   *specifies the environment size in n* bytes with values from 160 to 32768 (default = 160 bytes)

/p   causes the DOS command processor you start to become permanent

/c *string*   executes a following commandgiven by *string*

Example: command /c chkdsk a:

starts a new command processor under the current program, runs the chkdsk command on the disc in the A: drive, and returns to the first command processor.

comp   External, protected/real — compares two files and reports differences.

Example: comp file1 file2

copy [options]   Internal, protected/real — copies one or more files to specified disc. If preferred, copies can be given different names.

Option:

/a specifies an ASCII (text) file

/b specifies a binary file. When used with a source filename, it copies the entire file, including the end-of-file mark. When used with a target filename, it omits the end-of-file mark

/v causes the verification of data

54

Example: copy *.exe a:/v

copies all files with the .exe extension to the a: drive with verification.

date
: Internal, protected/real — enters or changes the current date.

del [option]
: Internal, protected/real — deletes all files with the designated filespec.

Option:
/p displays filenames to confirm deletion

Example: del a:*.txt

deletes all files which have the extension .txt from the a: drive.

detach
: Internal, protected — allows execution of an OS/2 command in background mode and allows user to continue with further OS/2 commands.

dir [options]
: Internal, protected/real — lists the files in a directory.

Options:
/p displays the directory list a page at a time
/w delects wide display

diskcomp
: External, protected/real — compares the contents of the disc in the source drive to the disc in the destination drive.

diskcopy
: External, protected/real — copies the contents of the disc in the source drive to the disc in the destination drive.

dpath
: External, protected — sets and displays the data-file path to be searched by external commands or batch files.

55

Example: dpath c:\;c:\comms

will search the root directory as well as the comms sub-directory in the c: drive.

endlocal   Internal, protected/real — works in conjunction with SETLOCAL command to preserve the current drive, directory and environment settings within a batch file to ensure that the batch file changes are only temporary.

exit   Internal, protected/real — exits the command processor and returns to a previous level.

fastopen [option]   External, real — store in memory the location of directories and recently opened files on a specified drive.

Option:
/x   allows use of expanded memory. If this option is used, then /x option must also be used with the **buffers** command

fdisk   External, protected/real — sets up and partitions the fixed disc for use with OS/2 and other operating systems. This command is also used to display and change the current active partition.

find [options]   External, protected/real — searches for a specific string of text in a specified ASCII file or files.

Options:
/c   prints the count of lines containing the string
/n   precedes each occurrence with the relative line number in the file
/v   displays all lines not containing the specified string

56

Example: find "lost words" chap1

searches for the string 'lost words' (which must appear within full quotes) in the named file (chap1).

format [options]   External, protected/real — formats the disc in the specified drive.

Options:

/4   formats a double-sided disc with 40 tracks, 9 sectors per track for 360 kB in a high capacity (1.2 MB) disc drive per track

/n   specifies the number of sectors per track, i.e. /n:9 for nine sectors

/t   specifies the number of tracks, i.e. /t:40 for forty tracks

/v   allows a volume label to be given to the disc

/s   copies the system files from the logged drive

Example: format a:/4/s

graftabl [nnn]   External, real — loads a custom designed, colour graphics font table into memory. It also supports the multilingual code page 850. The value for **nnn** is a three digit number, specifying the code page to be used.

help [options]   External, protected/real — provides additional help on each OS/2 error message.

Options:

ON   turns on the display of the help line

OFF   turns off the display of the help line

msg   specifies the message id for which additional information is required

join   External, real — joins a disc drive to a specific path.

keyb[xx]	External, protected — selects a special keyboard layout. Omitting **xx** returns the current status of the keyboard.
label	External, protected/real — creates or changes the volume identification label on a disc.
md (or mkdir)	Internal, protected/real — creates a new directory on the specified disc.
mode [options]	External, protected/real — sets the mode of operation on a display monitor, parallel/serial printer or the RS232C port. The keyboard repetition and autorepeat start delay time can be set. Also, it allows the setting of the number of rows to any of 25, 43 or 50 on the screen, and there is a wider range of serial-port configurations.

Options:
Display: mode [n,m]
where n can be:

40	sets display width to 40 characters per line
80	sets display width to 80 characters per line
bw40	sets screen to black and white display with 40 characters
bw80	sets screen to black and white display with 80 characters
co40	sets screen to colour display with 40 characters
co80	sets screen to colour display with 80 characters
mono	sets screen to monochrome with 80 characters

The value of m (number of rows to be displayed) can be set to 25, 43 or 50 depending on the display adapter attached, with the default value set at 25.

Example: mode co80,43

Printer: mode COMi: [n][,[m][,p]]
i   sets printer number with legal
    values from 1 to 3
n   sets number of characters per line
    with legal values of 80 or 132
m   sets the number of lines per inch
    with legal values of 6 or 8
p   allows continuous reentries on a
    time-out error

Example: mode LPT1: 132,8

sets the printer in the fist parallel port
to 132 characters per line and 8 lines
per inch.

Printer: mode COMi: [b][,p][,d][,s]
i   sets   an   asynchronous
    communications port number
    with legal values from 1 to 8
b   sets the baud (transmission rate)
    which may be 110, 1550, 300, 600,
    1200, 2400, 4800, 9600 or 19200
p   sets the parity. Its value can be: N
    (none), O (odd), E (even), M
    (mark), or S (space)
d   sets the databits which may be 5,
    6, 7, or 8 with the default set at 7
s   sets the stopbits which may be 1,
    1.5, or 2 with the default set at 2
    when b=110; otherwise the
    default is set at 1. Stopbits can be
    set to either 1 or 1.5 provided d=5

more   External, protected/real — reads data
                          from the standard I/O and sends
                          output to the console a screen-full at a
                          time.

                          Example: type read.me | more

                          displays the contents of the read.me
                          file one screen at a time.

patch [option]   External, protected/real — allows
                          changes to an executable file; it
                          provides a method for fixing a bug in
                          an executable file.

Option:

/a allows PATCH to execute in automatic mode and to obtain input from a file.

path
Internal, protected/real — sets and displays the path to be searched by external commands or batch files.

Example: path c:\;c:\os2;c:\comms

will search the root directory as well as the OS2 and COMMS sub-directories for files.

print [options]
External, protected/real — can be used to print text files in background mode, while other tasks are being performed. Using the command without options displays files already in the print queue.

Options:

/d specifies the print device such as PRN or LPTn (n=1 to 3)

/b causes Ctrl-Z characters encountered not to be interpreted as end-of-file indicators

/c cancels the currently printing file if the spool command is active

/t allows cancellation of files in print queue if the spool command is active

prompt
Internal, protected, real — changes the command prompt.

Example: pg

which allows the path of the current working directory to be displayed as the prompt.

rd (or rmdir)
Internal, protected/real — removes the specified directory.

recover	External, protected/real — recovers a file (minus the data in the bad sector) or the files on a disc can be recovered if the directory has been damaged.
ren (or rename)	Internal, protected/real — changes the file name.

Example: ren a:\docs\memo1 memo2

will rename the memo1 file, which is to be found in sub-directory docs on a disc in the a: drive, to memo2.

replace [options]	External, protected/real — allows easy updating of files from a source disc to a target disc of files having the same name.

Options:
/a also adds files that exist on the source disc but not on the target disc
/p prompts the user before replacing
/r replaces read only files
/s searches all directories of the target disc drive. /a and /s cannot be used together
/w waits for disc insertion in drive before beginning search

restore [options]	External, protected/real — restores one or more files that were backed up using the 'backup' command.

Options:
/m restores those files on the target disc that have been changed since the last backup
/n restores any files from the backup disc to the target disc if they do not exist on the target disc
/p prompts user before overwriting existing files by restoring
/s restores files in the specified directory and all files in any sub-directories of the specified directory

Example: restore A: C:*.* /S

restores all files on the backup discs, including sub-directories, from the A: drive to the C: drive.

set
Internal, protected/real — sets strings into the command processor's environment. The general form of the command is:

set [name=[parameter]]

Set by itself displays the current environment.

setcom40
External, real — sets the CPM port address so a DOS program can access the COM port interface directory to support a serial device, when the appropriate COM0n.SYS device driver has been installed.

setlocal
Internal, protected/real — preserves the current drive, directory and environment settings within a batch file. It works in conjunction with ENDLOCAL command. SETLOCAL saves the current settings that ENDLOCAL later restores.

sort [options]
External, protected/real — reads data from the console or a file, sorts it and sends it to the console or file.

Options:
/r sorts in reverse order

Example: dir | sort

sorts the output of the 'dir' command in alphabetical order.

spool
External, protected/real — allows initialization of the OS/2 print spooler for operations from multiple applications.

This print spooler supports only parallel devices (LPT1, LPT2, LPT3, and PRN) as input devices. Output devices can be parallel or serial devices such as COM1, COM2 and COM3. By specifying a parallel printer as the input device, redirection from a parallel printer port to a serial printer can be achieved.

start   Internal, protected — starts an OS/2 mode program in another session. Its primary use is to start programs at system startup. The special batch file, STARTUP.CMD, allow this to happen.

subst   External, protected/real — allows substitution of a virtual drive for an existing drive and path.

Example: subst e: a:\wproc\docs

will cause future reference to drive d: to be taken as replacement to the longer reference to a:\wproc\docs.

sys   External, protected/real — transfers the hidden operating system files from the logged drive to the disc in the specified drive.

time   Internal, protected/real — displays and sets the system time in a 12- or 24-hour format.

trace   External, protected/real — allows the tracing of system events, such as opening a file, writing to a file, or sending output to the display. The trace ON command must appear in the CONFIG.SYS file in order to activate it.

tree   External, protected/real — displays the directory structure graphically.

type   Internal, protected/real — displays the contents of a file on the VDU.

ver	Internal, protected/real — displays the OS/2 version number.
verify	Internal, protected/real — allows the verify switch to be turned ON or OFF.
	Example: verify=OFF
vol	Internal, protected/real — displays the disc volume label, if it exists.
xcopy [options]	External, protected/real — copies files and directories, including lower level sub-directories, if they exist, to the destination drive and directory.

Options:

/a copies source files that have their archive bit set

/d copies source files which were modified on or after a specified date

/e copies sub-directories even if they are empty — use this option in conjunction with the /s option

/m copies archived files only, but also turns off the archive bit in the source file

/p prompts the user with "(Y/N?)"

/s copies directories and their sub-directories unless they are empty

/v causes verification of each file as it is written

GLOSSARY OF TERMS

ASCII
: It is a binary code representation of a character set. The name stands for "American Standard Code for Information Interchange".

AUTOEXEC.BAT
: A batch file containing commands which are automatically executed on booting up the system.

BASIC
: A high level programming language. The name stands for "Beginner's All-purpose Symbolic Instruction Code".

BIOS
: The Basic Input/Output System. It allows the core of the operating system to communicate with the hardware.

Buffer
: RAM memory allocated to store data being read from disc.

Byte
: A grouping of binary digits (0 or 1) which represent information.

Cluster
: A unit of one or more sectors. It is the minimum amount of space that can be allocated to a file on disc.

CMD.COM
: The Operating System's Command line Processor for protected mode operations which analyzes what is typed at the keyboard and causes execution of the appropriate command.

COMMAND.COM
: Equivalent to CMD.COM, but for real mode operations.

CONFIG.SYS
: A special file that allows the system to be configured closer to requirement.

Directory
: An area on disc where information relating to a group of files is kept.

DOS
: The Disc Operating System. A collection of small specialised programs that allow interaction between user and computer.

FAT	The File Allocation Table. An area on disc where information is kept on which space on disc has been allocated to which file.
File	The name given to an area on disc containing a program or data.
Filespec	File specification made up of drive, path, filename and a three letter extension.
FORTRAN	A high level programming language. It stands for FORmula TRANslation.
Memory	Part of computer consisting of storage elements organised into addressable locations that can hold data and instructions.
Prompt	The System prompt displayed on screen (usually [C:\] in protected mode and C> in real mode).
RAM	Random Access Memory. The micro's volatile memory. Data held in it is lost when power is switched off.
ROM	Read Only Memory. The micro's non-volatile memory. Data are written into this memory at manufacture and are not affected by power loss.
Root	Directory The main disc directory under which a number of sub-directories can be created.
Sector	Disc space, normally 512 bytes long.
SHELL	A front end to the Operating System or an alternative Command Processor.
System	Short for computer system, implying a specific collection of hardware and software.
System Disc	A disc containing the hidden and command files of OS/2.

INDEX

NOTES